JONATHAN ADLER

on HAPPY CHIC
➳ Accessorizing

STERLING INNOVATION
An imprint of Sterling Publishing Co., Inc.

New York / London
www.sterlingpublishing.com

Acknowledgments

I am the luckiest potter/decorator/retailer/author in the world because I get to collaborate with the most creative, brilliant, and hilarious people. Thank you to...

- **Photographers:** Jessica Antola, Colleen Duffley, Evan Joseph, Joshua McHugh, Ngoc Minh Ngo, Thomas Olcott, Albert Sanchez, Todd Selby, Jonathan Skow, William Waldron, and Dan Wilby.

- **Clients:** Peri and Nacho Arenas, Adam and Denise, Liz Lange, Nanette Lepore and Bob Savage, Stan Parker and Jennifer Deppe Parker, Doug Teitelbaum, and Barbie.

- **Family:** Amy, David, Harry, Mom, my late father, and my favorite person on earth, Simon.

- **Sterling operatives:** Marcus Leaver, Jason Prince, Joelle Herr, Ashley Prine, and Melissa McKoy.

- **JA peeps:** Fearless Leaders: Gary Fuhrman, Erik Baker, and David Frankel. Those who worked on the book: Stephen Moss, Leslie Degler, Jerin Tueck, and Edwin Vera, and a thank you to the entire JA team, from the warehouse, the stores, the office, and the design studio.

- **And, finally, to the group that slaved away to create this book: Celia Fuller, Pam Horn, Jen Renzi, and the sublime Charlotte Hillman.**

STERLING, the Sterling logo, STERLING INNOVATION, and the Sterling Innovation logo are registered trademarks of Sterling Publishing Co., Inc.

Library of Congress Cataloging-in-Publication Data Available

10 9 8 7 6 5 4 3 2 1

Published by Sterling Publishing Co., Inc.
387 Park Avenue South, New York, NY 10016
© 2010 by Jonathan Adler
Distributed in Canada by Sterling Publishing
C/o Canadian Manda Group, 165 Dufferin Street
Toronto, Ontario, Canada M6K 3H6
Distributed in the United Kingdom by GMC Distribution Services
Castle Place, 166 High Street, Lewes, East Sussex, England BN7 1XU
Distributed in Australia by Capricorn Link (Australia) Pty. Ltd.
P.O. Box 704, Windsor, NSW 2756, Australia

Design by Celia Fuller
Cover photo © Colleen Duffley
Jonathan Adler Executive Editor: Charlotte Hillman

Sterling ISBN 978-1-4027-7430-0

For information about custom editions, special sales, premium and corporate purchases, please contact Sterling Special Sales Department at 800-805-5489 or specialsales@sterlingpublishing.com.

Contents

Foreword

Jonathan Adler grew up in a *mad, mod* white house in New Jersey. His parents, Cynthia and Harry, were practitioners of the art of eclectic decor.

Though modern and minimal, the entire house was filled with daring juxtapositions and eccentric installations. In the foyer, an orange Verner Panton umbrella stand rubbed shoulders with a giant folk-art-y carved-wood, bear-shaped coatrack; a cluster of '70s funk ceramics adorned the massive Albrizzi living room coffee table. Nearby, a wall of bookshelves was dotted with alternating clusters of Jonathan's teen pottery and his father's figurative sculptures.

The New Jersey *apple* does not fall far from the *tree.* Jonathan's childhood bedroom was accessorized with the same creative abandon.

Homemade puppets dangled above the bed. The Formica built-ins were artfully stuffed with Bowie albums and *Interview* magazines. And the window ledges were packed with Japanese vessels acquired at the annual Philadelphia Craft Show. And yes, there were childhood Snoopies and Trolls in the mix.

Having spent his adult life filling the world with decorative accessories, Jonathan now—being the well-brought-up Jersey boy that he is—feels an overwhelming obligation to **share the wisdom** gained from his *objet*-filled childhood and help us all to integrate and arrange the objects and accessories that life brings our way...

...and, most importantly, to do it with creative expression and a sense of enjoyment.

Happy tablescaping!

LOVE, SIMON DOONAN

Bohemian collector: Fashion designer Nanette Lepore is visually sophisticated enough to handle a quirky mix in her lair. The pieces that we chose for her New York home—a Berber carpet, a Moroccan table, a Napoleonic bust—shouldn't gel but somehow do, precisely because they're so personal.

INTRODUCTION
Happy Chic Your Home

My decorating philosophy stems from a contradiction. On one hand, I'm obsessed with design rigor—with making interiors that are impeccably chic and with crafting timeless, tasteful products that your heirs will fight over. And yet! The relentless pursuit of tastefulness is a rather empty endeavor. There's an anonymity to it that I find distressing. Where's the fun? Where's the heart? Where's the *joie de vivre?*

The best quote ever concerning the topic of chic was uttered by the late Sir Hardy Amies, couturier to Queen Elizabeth II of England, who always dressed the monarch in practical silhouettes and relatable looks. When asked why he didn't tart her up in more *au courant* attire, Amies replied that there's something "cold and cruel" to chic—a not-so-friendly side that's snobbish and exclusive. Her Majesty knows not to overdo the snootiness; so should we all.

I believe chic should be accessible, and that the key to achieving accessibility is injecting your personality. My antidote to tired tastefulness is to lay the foundation of good decorating and then punctuate with a dash of levity. Just a dash! Too much tastefulness is pompous and dull, but too much spirited fun is tacky. For guidance, I offer the following fail-safe formula, derived from years of sociological inquiry and data crunching:

95% CHIC + 5% HAPPY = THE DECORATIVE NIRVANA THAT I CALL HAPPY CHIC

That five percent is a small portion. Yet it's the most crucial—and the hardest to nail. Said dash of levity should be quirky but not wacky, kicky but not kitschy.

Graphic élan: Bold yellow and gray striped bedding gets an extra jolt from a single black pillow—echoed by the needlepoint "love" that cushions the baroque club chair nearby.

Girly glam: With its tufted-velvet pouf, leopard-print dressing chair, and mirrored vanity, Nanette Lepore's boudoir is kittenish and glamorous—very her. Whether you swing understated or over-the-top, your inner sanctum should reflect your inner diva!

Brit wit: My bloke Simon's home office channels his personality. The decor is about gentlemanly-ness and proper Britishness, but also about irreverence: Note the Union Jack in shocking color combos.

"FLOAT"
FURNISHINGS
IN THE CENTER
OF A ROOM.
THE SPACE
WILL FEEL MORE
OPEN AND LESS
OBSCURED.

Personalize your pad: When Simon isn't writing, he's dressing windows. Thus the mannequin heads everywhere—which make great centerpieces for quirky scapes.

The goals of this introduction are:

➥ to teach you the rules of decorating

➥ to teach you how to break them.

Herewith, my three-point plan for Happy Chic-ifying your home:

Step one: FIND YOUR LOOK. Create a personal decorating mission statement—a catchphrase to guide your every design decision.

Step two: FOLLOW THE PRINCIPLES OF ARRANGING. Whether arranging a house or accessorizing a tableau, you have the same basic tools in your arsenal: scale, shape, color, and content. Use them!

Step three: BEND THE RULES! Let formal rigor become a springboard for play. Being pitch-perfect is a matter of throwing in an off-note.

*turn the page
to get started!*

ACCESSORIZE EVERY SURFACE. EVEN A RADIATOR PROVIDES A DISPLAY OPPORTUNITY. CLUSTERED CERAMICS ARE A GREAT WAY TO DISGUISE VENTS; THEY STAND UP TO HEAT WHILE STILL LETTING AIR FLOW.

FIND YOUR LOOK

When it comes to decorating, I like to switch it up. Why saddle yourself with one particular shtick when you can draw on various established styles? Here are three of the recurring "looks" that predominate my own oeuvre:

- *Wasp-y Chic* is all about patrician panache, crisp geometries, and twinkly materials: think nickel nailheads and rich lacquer. Get the look by layering in a dollop of irony and lightheartedness, but not so much as to be irreverent.
- ***Playful Pop*** is a little bit naughty and a lot of fun: Clear colors and pared-back forms like Parsons tables combine to woo the crowd with saucy wit. Playful Pop is like the love child of Jean-Michel Frank and Farrah Fawcett, imbuing classic decorating with '70s sex appeal.
- ORGANIC MODERN Think mid-century modernism on an herbal-tea bender: handcrafted furnishings and rustic textures punctuated with strokes of color and metallic accents so the effect is earthy but not crunchy.

Wasp-y Chic

Muses: LILLY PULITZER, BABE PALEY, JACKIE O.

Inspirational locations: PALM BEACH, SUTTON PLACE, TROUSDALE

Color palette: CHARTREUSE, WHITE, GOLD

Signature *objets*: CHINESE CHIPPENDALE CHAIRS, NEEDLEPOINT, BACKGAMMON SET

Playful Pop

Muses: ANDY WARHOL, JOE COLOMBO, COURRÈGES, VERNER PANTON

Inspirational locations: BRASILIA, SWINGING LONDON

Color palette: ORANGE, MAGENTA, SILVER

Signature *objets*: EERO SAARINEN CHAIR, PANTON LAMP

ORGANIC MODERN

Muses: TALITHA GETTY, ALI MCGRAW, JADE JAGGER

Inspirational locations: BIG SUR, IBIZA, TOPANGA CANYON

Color palette: TEAL, CINNAMON, CHOCOLATE, CHAMBEIGE

Signature *objets*: MOROCCAN BERBER RUG, C. JERE SCULPTURE, MACRAMÉ OWL

WORKBOOK
What do you want your home to say about you?

The objects you surround yourself with at home should be interesting and special. They need to express something about you and communicate that something to the world. Start with a psychological exercise: Ask yourself what you want your home to declare. That you have a bohemian spirit? That you are upwardly mobile? That you are a celebutante-worshipping funster? Mull, ponder, and stew. Now jot down a list of ten words that describe what you want to communicate about yourself through your decorating scheme. Be emboldened! Nobody's reading this page but you.

1.

2.

3.

4.

5.

6.

7.

8.

9.

10.

Express yourself! Whether you like surrounding yourself with chintz or chrome, Louis XIV or LeRoy Neiman, *I want you to be your-self—and be happy.*

15

THE PRINCIPLES OF ARRANGING

Decorating is like cooking a meal. Say, for instance, you have beef and onions in your fridge. If you are feeling French and fussy, you might envision Boeuf Bourguignon à la Julia Child. If you're craving something Asian, you'd crack open your stir-fry cookbook and toss some bok choy into the mix. And if you have White Castle on the brain, you might scour cyberspace for an onion ring recipe and mince the beef to make burgers. ***The same ingredients + 3 recipes = 3 totally different meals!*** This applies to decorating, too. Although your ingredients are always the same:

Density: Packing it in emphasizes both the similarities (content, colors) and differences (shapes, scales) among these pieces of pottery, creating a balanced display.

↬ SCALE is the visual weight or size of objects in relation to one another—and to their surroundings.

↬ SHAPE encompasses the form, profile, and proportions of a piece.

↬ Choosing objects in the same COLOR family is an easy way to establish order!

↬ The notion of CONTENT—that inanimate objects have the capacity to communicate meaning—is one of the most under-considered aspects of design.

WHEN ARRANGING
FRONTAL COMPOSITIONS
(SEE PAGE 21), PLACE
THE TALLEST ITEM
IN BACK AND THE
SMALLEST UP FRONT.

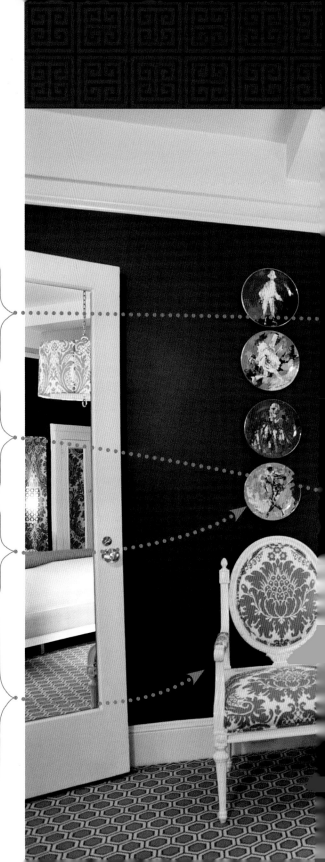

Scale, shape, color, and content are the tried and true ingredients for composing objects and furnishing vignettes. How do these factors come into play in my master bedroom? Let's break it down!

↝ **SCALE** This vignette showcases a range of scales and proportions. A giant screen brings grandeur while small accessories echo the colors and motifs.

↝ **SHAPE** Because I chose leggy Louis chairs, I wanted a desk with an unobtrusive base and a very different profile. Always curate a mix of legs and bases for furniture.

↝ **COLOR** The orange textiles, brown wall paint, and patterned blue carpet reiterate the hues featured on the multicolored wall-hung plates.

↝ **CONTENT** The elements here are quite traditional: classic Louis chairs, a symmetrical arrangement, brocades, plates hung on a wall. But the content derives from the unexpected elements like the giant banana sculpture and the jolt of orange, which conspire to add pop to this vignette.

Look down: A giant banana sculpture below the desk brings dramatic flair to a typically forgotten little nook.

ARRANGING 101: A VISUAL GUIDE

So, I corralled some curios to demonstrate how to choose objects that work together—and how to array them into gorgeous groupings. It can be daunting to figure out where to begin when faced with a pile of favorite *objets* and lots of empty tabletops. But fear not: a certain logic underlies decorating. Making pottery taught me how to accessorize and arrange anything. It forced me to figure out what qualities comprise a good piece—and how to display those pieces in stores. For homes, I just apply those same principles, only on a different scale.

Artful design is all in the balance.

For arranging, this means juxtaposing silhouettes and colors, and even ideas and concepts against each other in a jaunty play of genre: highlight differences between pieces or draw attention to their similarities.

Start by establishing framing.

Items in a room or on a surface should be composed as you would paint a canvas, with scale, sequencing, and balance conceived from one specific vantage point. Consoles, bookshelves, and artworks are generally viewed from a *frontal perspective*, while furnishings such as dining room tables and coffee tables are viewed *in the round* and should be accessorized accordingly.

SYMMETRY

Most people think the word *symmetry* means *mirror* image: two identical lamps placed on either end of a console, for instance. But to me, symmetry is about highlighting likenesses between things, and can thus be achieved by pairing two objects with a similar sense of scale, proportion, or color to create a calming, organized effect.

➽ Blue glass lamps anchor both ends of the white dresser. Although the lamps are different sizes, symmetry comes through the repeated color.

➽ I balanced the different lamp heights by pairing the taller one with a shorter cluster of objects—and vice versa.

➽ Hang plates in unusual locations to fill up empty wall space and round out compositions, adding decoration and detail without usurping surface area.

➽ The focal point of this tableau is actually the smallest item: the tiny dot of *yellow* from the centrally placed vase.

I USED COASTERS TO GIVE SOME OF THE VASES A LITTLE MORE HEIGHT.

Remove book jackets to make spines look harmonious!

ASYMMETRY

While symmetry is achieved by emphasizing the similarity between adjacent objects, *asymmetry* is about underscoring the differences between them to establish a *lively sense of rhythm.* In design, being pitch-perfect is a matter of throwing in an off-note; the trick is to create a dynamic balance of different scales, proportions, and colors.

❦ Here, I grouped numerous items into a series of little moments: one book is propped up vertically, like the paintings on the wall; a stack of plates adds height to a bud vase; another vase gets a lift from a Lucite box.

⚓ Bestow a deliberately ad hoc quality by unevenly grouping objects of different heights and shapes.

⚓ Artful scaping is about balancing opposites to create dynamic *tension* and *frisson*: Pair huge with tiny, rustic with refined, prim with louche.

⚓ Half of the tableau is arranged symmetrically; the other half is asymmetrical. Look at the overall composition, but break it down into constituent parts.

WORKBOOK
Filling in the gaps

Take inventory of your go-to accessories—the ones you'll use to start scaping.

1.

2.

3.

4.

5.

6.

7.

8.

9.

10.

BEND THE RULES

Conformity is a bore! Acts of concerted and deliberate rebellion are the foundation of personal stylishness. Arranging and accessorizing in the Happy Chic vein is like that maxim about getting dressed and then taking off just one bauble before walking out the door. The decorative equivalent is to establish a perfectly resolved room, artfully arrayed tableau, or expertly styled floral arrangement—and then mess with it just a bit. In other words, aim for put-togetherness and then tweak, tweak, tweak to brand it with your imprimatur. It's much easier to subtract from studied perfection than to add up to artful *dishabille*.

Your new mantra: *classical foundation, playful punctuation!*

Ménage à trois:
This assemblage of gold vases demonstrates how well three-somes can work.

MU*S*e

Verner Panton

THE KING OF POP

⮕ Before there was Michael Jackson, there was Verner Panton.

⮕ He was an *enfant terrible* who broke free from the anal retention of Danish design.

⮕ He did insanely modern stuff half a century ago that makes today's new design look dusty and old.

⮕ He brought *psychedelia* into the home.

⮕ He created radical squishy environments that defined the term *"groovy pad."*

⮕ He gave your butt the S chair. Say *thank you!*

⮕ He made twinkly sequined light fixtures that look like they came from another planet.

⮕ He embraced plastic.

⮕ He wallowed in *COLOR.*

⮕ *Long live the King!*

A peaceful tableau: A tight cluster of pottery, books, and flora elevates a marble side table to the status of pedestal for sculptural presentation.

IN THE ROUND
Tablescapes

Tables come in so many shapes and sizes—nesting, stacking, coffee, dining—each providing a vastly different canvas for creative experimentation. The trick to Happy Chic tablescaping is continued fussing and improvisation. Slave and slave and slave to get things just right! Arranging objects is an ***art***, but it's also a ***science***. Start by arraying things in an orderly fashion, situating the big stuff and then layering in color echoes and unexpected items. Once everything is properly positioned, be sure to keep screwing it up a little bit so it doesn't feel too labored or *done*—even if you've killed yourself to get it just so.

Reading room? Do you use *your* dining room table? Even if you're a serious home chef, chances are good that you use your table—and the dining room itself—infrequently. In this New York penthouse, we treated the dining room table as a library, displaying a range of books and accessories to balance the grandeur with a casual feel.

HELMUT

Juxtaposition of scale:
In my SoHo boutique, here is a lively range of scale and an eclectic mix of objects: earthy pots, a twinkly starburst, and a miniature bronze bull.

ONE TABLE, TWO WAYS

Here are two templates for arranging a coffee table:

One: I arrayed enameled bowls of alternating colors in a row along the edge of the table, and then I softened the lines with an asymmetrical trio of stacked books. A vase rounds out the composition, anchoring the far end.

Two: To achieve a simpler look, I grouped the bowls into a circular pattern that shows off their petal-like form and reconfigured the stack of books into a pedestal for the flowers. *Presto!*

Symmetry + tweak = asymmetry: A pair of squirrel ring boxes face off in front of a colorful Rex Ray painting. The symmetrical arrangement is wittily undermined by the removal of one of the acorn tops, instilling a sassy bit of rebellion.

Collect and cluster! A range of candlesticks of different shapes and sizes animates this tablescape.

CANDLELIGHT FLATTERS THE FACE, ERASING FINE LINES AND WRINKLES! YOUR DINNER GUESTS WILL THANK YOU.

Happy color: I based the design of this tabletop on my Bargello diamond needlepoint pillow, rendering the pattern in glass mosaic for a weatherproof "tablecloth."

37

Weird works: Design around the things you love, no matter how odd or idiosyncratic they might be. This vintage Brutalist owl sculpture provides the focal point for a cocktail table in my New York apartment.

Mix big and small: Here, an oversized owl presides over a little Saarinen table in my New York bedroom.

BTW, I have a soft spot for owls: This is a sampling of my own owl creations.

Surprise me! In fashion designer Liz Lange's New York foyer, the color scheme and spirit were restrained until we plonked down a bright orange table as a focal point. Use tables to create a sculptural moment for surfaces on which you'd never normally place anything with a functional purpose.

Anything goes: I have placed a simple tree trunk as a side table to crank up the Surrealism in my New York powder room. Incongruous objects of varying scales complement the trippy Fornasetti chair and the bold brocade wallpaper. Try thinking out of the box. You can achieve this look too.

DOLLS

FESTOON TABLES WITH FLOWERS!

more flowers

Flower-musing: Bud vases are to flowers as Hamburger Helper is to ground beef: they stretch a simple bouquet into a slew of floral moments.

WHEN IT COMES TO ARRANGING FLOWERS, I FOLLOW ONE SIMPLE RULE: CREATE ABUNDANT, TIGHT CLUSTERS OF ALL THE SAME BLOOMS OR COLORS.

more flowers

PANSY

MAGNOLIA

CHERRY BLOSSOMS

TULIP

POPPY

ANEMONES

DAFFODIL

GARDENIA

ZINNIA

PEONY

AMARYLLIS

DAHLIA

SUNFLOWER

WHITE ROSE

GERBER DAISY

DAISY

BRANCHES

CALENDULA

RANUNCULUS

WORKBOOK

These are my go-to flowers for each season. Pick your favorites!

Early Spring

Pansies

Magnolias

Cherry blossom branches

Anemones

Spring

Tulips

Poppies

Daffodils

Zinnias

Summer

Gardenias

Peonies

Amaryllis

White roses

Sunflowers

Dahlias

Fall

Gerber daisies

Regular old daisies

Calendulas

Winter

Branches

Ranunculus

WORKBOOK

*What type of blossoms
make you bloom?*

Set the mood: On Liz Lange's kitchen island, a big yellow bouquet establishes a happy, sunny mood. Flowers make a great decorative motif, too. The poppy, abstracted floral fabric of the drum shade and the Cherner chair seats brings the outdoors in.

A madcap jumble: Cheeky needlepoint pillows create an anything-goes vibe in the guest room of my Palm Beach getaway.

THE SOFT STUFF
Pillowscapes

Nothing says luxury like a squishy pillow and fluffy throw. Sink into ***softness*** for the ultimate in ***pampering!*** But scaping all that soft stuff—beds, upholstered chairs, *tête-à-têtes*—can be a bit tricky. Use pillows as punctuation, not the main event, adding a dose of color and playfulness. An immoderate pile on your sofa has the opposite of its intended effect: it's totally off-putting! Exuberance should come through the riotous patterns and sly, witty design of the pillows themselves. And be sure to change the scheme periodically. Replacing pillows is an inexpensive way to transform the look of a room.

Herewith, more tips for squishifying your pad.

I KEPT THE LAYOUT OF PILLOWS SIMPLE HERE SINCE THE BED SITS IN A COZY, COCOONING NOOK LINED IN PADDED UPHOLSTERY.

BEDSCAPES

TAKE A CUE FROM THIS PILLOW ARRANGEMENT, WHICH PAIRS VOLUPTUOUSNESS AND RIGOR VIA CRISP LAYERING.

- **Back layer:** A trio of square shams picks up the lampshade color.

- **Next layer:** Pillows for sleeping. These are a little shorter than the pillows with shams, but extend a tad wider so the composition of the whole doesn't get too pyramidal.

- **Next layer:** A pair of decorative pillows in a juicy pink that echoes the picture above.

- **Front layer:** An insouciant trio of throw pillows arranged in an asymmetrical jumble. These feature the most decorative fabric, but the neutral color keeps them from looking too *too*.

> A SURREAL FORNASETTI PLATE ALWAYS WORKS ABOVE A BED!

Harmonious hues: Decorating with items in the same color palette allows you to mix up pattern and size so an asymmetrical array can rule the day, while a mix of color—like the bed on the facing page—demands a more deliberate color composition.

Let the bedspread do the talking: I floated a giant Paul Evans mirrored four-poster in the middle of my Palm Beach bedroom, tempering its modernist rigor with ethnic exuberance in the form of a suzani tapestry (and the wisdom of a naughty Norwich terrier). The bed pillows get stashed in a closet during the day—just like hotel turndown service!

All-white bedding: In this young girl's room the color comes from the drapes used to frame the beds and is punctuated by riotously patterned, oversized pillows in needlepoint patchwork.

Neutral bedding: You'll have more license to play with accent pillows, but neutral doesn't have to mean all white; this bed celebrates the pleasing crispness of a judicious stroke of black, echoed by a needlepoint pillow.

Water view: This room has an airy, dreamy vibe consonant with the surreal majesty of its beachside Palm Beach locale. A blue throw the exact color of the water just steps outside forms a strong graphic element, breaking up the big white expanse of sofa.

AN ODE TO THE *tête-à-tête* SOFA

Oh, the genius of *tête-à-tête*! The style, designed to accommodate two people sitting face to face, facilitated courtship during Victorian times. But its prim provenance aside, there's something about a double-sided sofa that's just plain fun. It's a twist on a classic—making something formal seem less so. Since a *tête-à-tête* has two "fronts," I like to use it in the center of a room, as a hinge between two seating vignettes.

Blue mood: Convert a window ledge into an upholstered banquette for extra seating—a space-saver in a pint-sized breakfast nook. Keep the seat cushion tailored (sans tufting or trims) and choose a bold color that ties in to the surrounding decor.

PILLOWS ARE THE
exclamation point
OF THE HOME.

Take a shine to metals: I made a wall of handcrafted tile glazed in real platinum for the entryway of this Manhattan penthouse. Quietly reinforcing the glamour, a white Chinoiserie cabinet supports a soothingly symmetrical tableau.

FULL FRONTAL
Consoles, Shelves, and Mantels

I implore you to consider the manifold brilliance of the console table. *First*, it is an eminently practical piece, adept at squeezing into snug slivers of square footage like hallways and landings, and lending a furnished look to those in-between spaces while offering much-needed storage for assorted odds and ends. *Second* a console's narrow top surface is a perfect pedestal for the artful presentation of life-enhancing tchotchkes and meaningful objects. As with shelves and mantels, its lengthy dimensions are ideally suited to symmetrical compositions, which invite order and resolution—and who couldn't use more of that in their Happy Chic life?

MAKING AN ENTRANCE

T he foyer of my New York apartment is a *Playful Pop paean* to the versatility of consoles—and a lesson in how to arrange and accessorize them. Let's break it down!

⟿ **Scale:** Consoles are typically viewed frontally. Speak to the elongated proportions by anchoring both ends with strong pieces with equal visual heft. Just a few elements dominate this consolescape: a pair of bird bowls and an oversized gold vase.

⟿ **Shape:** With its square legs, lacquered finish, and unfussy lines, this console is a streamlined piece that mixes well with other genres and furniture styles, and functions as a tabula rasa for an ever-changing tableau of more curvaceous pieces.

⟿ **Color:** Orange and gold provide a sense of fun glamour. Minimalist scaping lets the color be the main event.

⟿ **Content:** Framed in two-by-fours, this looking glass is a funky take on a formal sunburst mirror. I love stashing stools below a console, and the Philippe Starck gnomes never fail to provide a chuckle.

Pop traditional: Liz Lange's nineteenth-century farmhouse gets a dose of pizzazz from the go-go white floors and the black ebonized doors. The mock-croc console is casually scaped to match the easy-breezy spirit of the house.

PLAY! **PROP ITEMS ON STACKED BOOKS AND PICK ACCESSORIES WITH A SENSE OF HUMOR AND FLAIR.**

Minimalist scaping: A pair of my shiny aorta vases was all I needed to play up the futuristic twinkle of this vintage Breuton console in the foyer of a New York townhouse. The louche '70s design tempers the seriousness of the white marble paneling, while the altar-like shape introduces a churchlike vibe cheekily echoed by the contemporary artwork by Erika Rothenberg above.

WEEK OF JAN. 4, 2100

**EVENINGS AT 7
IN THE PARISH HALL**

MON ABUSED SPOUSES
—ALL GENDERS WELCOME

TUE ALCOHOLICS ANONYMOUS

WED SINGLES SUPPORT GROUP:
FINDING LOVE ON
OTHER PLANETS

THU ANTI-HATE COALITION

FRI SOUP KITCHEN

SAT PARENTING YOUR CLONE

**SUNDAY SERMON
9 A.M.**

"ANOTHER CENTURY
OF PROGRESS"

Foyers + mirrors = Happy Chic:
In my Palm Beach apartment, a faceted octagonal mirror and splay-legged vintage console have a shared sensibility.

EXPLOIT FLOOR SPACE TO DISPLAY YOUR FAVORITE BITS! A GROUP OF POTS UNDER A TABLE LENDS HAPPY INSOUCIANCE.

Don't overlook nooks: Wall-mounted shelves make great space fillers. Take advantage of little nooks to hang a floating cabinet, as we did in this art connoisseur's entrance hall.

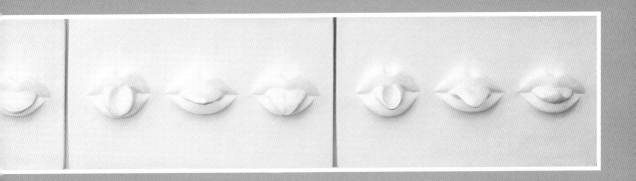

I MADE THESE PORCELAIN TONGUES AS TRIPPY, PROVOCATIVE DRAWER PULLS.

Wit is a crucial part of life: This cornucopia of pottery on the windowsill of my dining room is ruled by a giant '60s Italian ceramic king that always makes me smile as I eat my Apple Jacks.

Let artwork own the wall:
In this loft, natural materials and quiet colors—a rustic console, macramé jute rug, rough-hewn pottery—get a jolt of dynamism from the wall sculpture above: a '60s C. Jere sunburst.

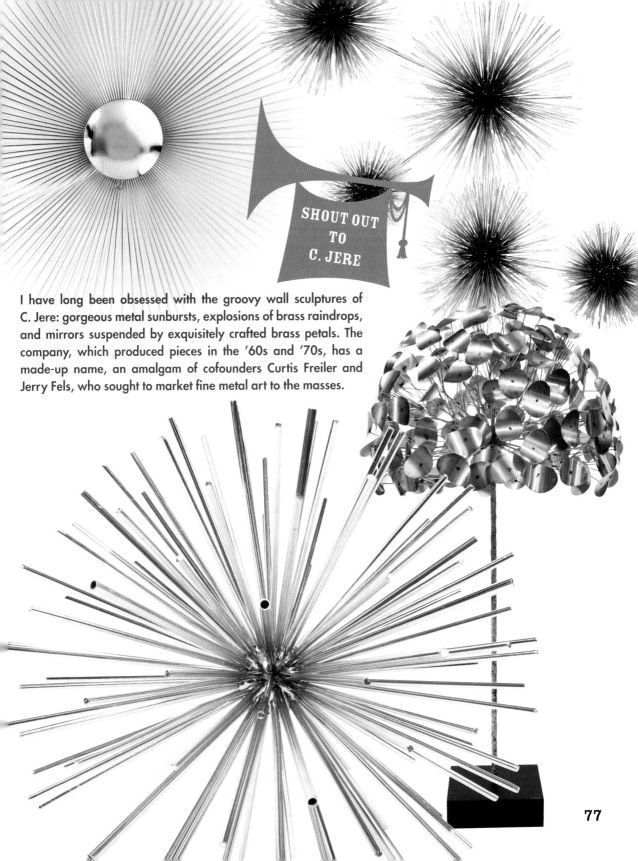

I have long been obsessed with the groovy wall sculptures of C. Jere: gorgeous metal sunbursts, explosions of brass raindrops, and mirrors suspended by exquisitely crafted brass petals. The company, which produced pieces in the '60s and '70s, has a made-up name, an amalgam of cofounders Curtis Freiler and Jerry Fels, who sought to market fine metal art to the masses.

Repetition rules:
A mantel's skinny dimensions are well suited to a row of accessories, like this collection of glass head figurines in my New York apartment.

Look up! People fixate on arranging everything at eye level, but being attentive to all surfaces—from the floor to the ceiling—gives your eye places to roam and makes a space look coherent and resolved. I love to plonk stuff atop a tall dresser or cabinet—like this Gothic gem—to create the illusion of more head room.

VISAGES
HUMANIZE
INANIMATE
OBJECTS. EVERY
ARRANGEMENT
NEEDS A FOCAL
POINT, AND
FACES ARE MY
SUREFIRE FAVES.

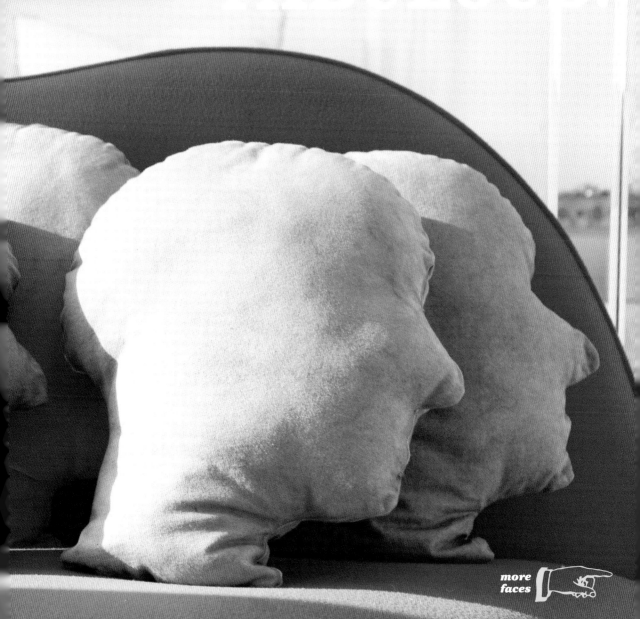

FACES ARE FABULOUS!

more
faces

Save face: Anchor a vignette with a face—or three! Use anthropomorphic forms like a Neoclassical bust, a cheeky vase, or an animal head to add instant grandeur and to bring a smile to *your* face.

KOONS

SIONS

BY DIAN HANSON

TASCHEN

WALL SHELVES ARE TYPICALLY USED FOR STORING BOOKS, BUT YOU CAN ALSO PUT THEM TO USE AS PEDESTALS FOR DISPLAYING YOUR FAVORITE ART AND OBJECTS.

LEAN ART EVERYWHERE—
EVEN ON SHELVES—TO CREATE
A PERSONAL, CASUAL VIBE.

Top shelf: Have a random nook or empty shelf to spare? Why not transform it into a bar by lining it with trippy wallpaper and filling it with more booze than you think you'll ever need? Nothing says "fun!" quite like a bar full of booze.

THE ANATOMY OF A
BOOKSHELF

Bookshelves can prove particularly vexing when it comes to accessorizing. Straightforward rows of books are probably the easiest to style; a random, haphazard mix of spine heights and color works best. Intermingling artworks and objects within is much trickier. Here's a quick primer on how to pull it off with panache, and look well-read *and* well-designed in the process.

1
Vertical vs. horizontal: Alternating standing and stacked tomes begets a more animated and dynamic look than an uninterrupted row.

2
Balance: A sculpture on both stacks gives this grouping a feeling of order.

3
Seize a tchotchke moment: This zebra acts a sort of reverse bookend, a pause *in media res* that helps keep standing tomes vertical.

4
Intersperse art: Small framed canvases surprise within the context of a bookshelf where you can enjoy them more intimately. Place at eye level and seem more cultured than you are.

Small groupings: To keep the look light, limit rows and stacks to just ten or twelve books.

5

Crowning: Place big objects on the hard-to-reach topmost shelf. They are pleasing to the eye—and don't need to be easily accessible.

6

Disrespect the shelf: Don't be afraid to let items dangle.

7

Hidden artwork: Although conventional wisdom dictates giving artwork pride of place, it's totally fine to place a piece so that it peeks out from behind a stack of horizontally stacked books.

8

An airy collection: Gives the shelf room to breathe.

9

Solo stack: Set off one stack in the middle of a shelf, bookended by free-standing sculptures on either side.

10

THIS "CABINET" IS ACTUALLY A RADIATOR COVER! THE CHICKEN WIRE AND FABRIC PANELING—USED IN LIEU OF SOLID DOORS—ENABLES THE RADIATOR TO BREATHE.

WHEN IN DOUBT, HANG FABRIC *throughout!*

Covert clutter: Cabinet doors inset with fabric panels are a feature I've repeated throughout my abode, from my den to my bedroom. This is a brilliantly easy way to hide clutter and add graphic punch. Back glass doors with a stretch of fabric, or pop out panels and replace with yardage.

MUSE

Talitha Getty

➥ She was born in Java, Indonesia, and spent time in a Japanese prisoner-of-war camp.

➥ When she married John Paul Getty Jr., she wore a white miniskirt trimmed with mink.

➥ She hung out with Mick and Marianne and Jimi.

➥ She was so *gorgeous* and *groovy* she almost turned Rudolf Nureyev straight.

➥ She became YSL's muse and introduced him to the intoxicating delights of Marrakesh.

➥ She invented international *bohemian glamour.*

➥ She died of a heroin overdose at the age of thirty.

➥ R.I.P., *queen* of the rich hippies.

Art crawling up the wall: This kind of installation is a looser riff on a salon-style configuration that takes advantage of vertical slivers of space.

ON THE WALL
Artwork

Collecting and displaying artwork is one of the most effective means of injecting Happy Chic personality into a home. Everyone's definition of "fine art" is a little different. Some like Wyeth; others prefer Warhol. ***To each his (or her) own!***

As for how to arrange your finery, I favor two extremes: meandering, salon-like installations and tight, repetitious grids. Collections of the same things don't always have to be grouped together, though; they can be threaded throughout your house to create continuity. Rehang regularly to enjoy your pieces in new contexts.

Art off the wall: Seek out unexpected places for art, even in traditional settings. The Manhattan penthouse of artist Jennifer Deppe Parker and her husband, Stan, has a wall of windows, forcing us to get creative about art-hanging opportunities. Jennifer's own painting is mounted from the ceiling with fishing wire. And the Takashi Murakami piece floats in the center of the room courtesy of an Arteluce easel lamp. Wall-hung plates are a great trick for a column, which demands small-scale pieces.

TIPS FOR AN *artful* SALON WALL

Covering an entire wall—or several walls—with a joyful hodgepodge of pieces is one of the most effective ways to inject liveliness and make the most of limited space. Many professional art installers have trouble with salon-like installations since they have an instinct for more precise arrangements; this is a situation where an untrained eye works to your advantage! The beauty of an allover installation is that a random, asymmetrical arrangement works best. The whole idea is to **not stress about the rules.** Take a cue from this mind-bending mélange of wall-to-wall works.

- **Planning:** Map out placement on the floor or cut out paper templates and tape them to the wall, moving things around until you settle on the most pleasing layout. Think of the ensemble as one big artwork; sketch an outline and arrange individual components within.

- **Composition:** Start at the center and work outward, leaving roughly even spacing between pieces. The more disparate the artworks, the better! Balance size and frame weight, alternating big and small, vertical and horizontal, to create rhythm and balance.

- **Vignettes:** Strike a bold note by grouping a few pieces together within a larger swath of artworks—an effect created by positioning the frames a little closer to each other.

- **Placement:** Go floor-to-ceiling or group objects loosely in the center of the wall. Just beware of hanging too low or right above a sofa, where a canvas might get jostled.

- **Integration:** Rather than stress about navigating art around your decor, incorporate furnishings like lampshades and even TVs into the composition. Hide your flatscreen in plain sight by surrounding it with canvases.

Go for the grid: A gridlike installation works best for art with same-size frames. Consistent spacing in between offers the tidiest look; depending on how much room you have—just enough for a little breathing room, but not so much that artworks appear unrelated.

Front and center: For small or oddly shaped pieces, go for a side-by-side series, like these marquetry clowns that I purchased in Italy. When mixing pieces that are differently sized or shaped, hang so that the center of each piece forms a continuous horizontal line—or align the edges of frames.

Fashion frame-up: In this little girl's room, we framed her mother's collection of playful Prada totes to create an art installation.

One of a kind: I crafted a grouping of glazed ceramic teardrops to fill a wall above the tufted leather sofa in my Palm Beach pied-à-terre. Mixing different scales and colors creates a lively composition.

naughty but

I NEED MORE

Neon rules! We made this illuminated sculpture to fit the space between two windows in my client's living room. The sassy sentiment, "naughty but nice," perfectly captures the spirit of the resident funsters.

Don't be afraid: Paint directly on your walls. I commissioned my friend Don Carney to create this pipe "painting"—very Magritte!—for the pocket door leading from my library up to my boudoir.

Wink wink: I am *obsessed* with eyeball-themed artworks and have them sprinkled all over my house. I think of them as talismans to ward away evil spirits. These were painted by my friend John-Paul Philippe; we gave him an assignment—do something "eye-ish"—and he delivered.

Don't revere windows! When confronted with a window that admits little light or faces a brick wall—like those in my New York living room slash ping-pong parlor—consider hanging art over the mullions. *Voilà:* instant view! I love that these paintings stare at me as I walk in—and remind me to keep my eye on the ball.

MORE *Happy Chic ideas* FOR ARRANGING ARTWORK

1 If you don't have the budget to collect schmancy artwork, think small—even collections of salt and pepper shakers make great little sculptures.

2 Frame a flatscreen TV so it looks less jarring and hideous. I love to use a bling-y silver leaf frame.

3 If you have a small sliver of wall, place a sculptural chair for instant art!

4 Don't forget to put art in the bathroom—just be careful with anything that might be damaged by moisture. Ceramic busts are a perfect choice.

5 We hung these newspaper sculptures by Donna Rosenthal in my client's walk-in closet as an irreverent nod to her couture collection.

6 Easels are a great way to display smaller solo works, and a genius means of circumventing limited wall space.

7 Art can appear anywhere, as shown on this Cindy Sherman dishware.

3

4

5

WORKBOOK

*Use this grid to map out the
configuration of your own salon
wall or art installation.*

Size matters: Ratchet up the drama by letting a single overscaled artwork—the bolder the better—take center stage and become the decorative focal point of a room or a seating vignette. Here, I hung a 1965 painting by the brilliant American Pop Surrealist Sante Graziani right over the moldings. When hanging art, the midpoint should be at eye level. Avoid the common mistake of mounting too high, especially in living or dining spaces where you're mostly viewing pieces while sitting down.

MU*S*e
Fleur Cowles

Her cultural influence far outlasted the print run of her inimitable magazine *Flair*. Published from February 1950 to January 1951, *Flair* covered the full swath of **highbrow** pursuits, from literature and travel to fine art and interior design, and included contributions by Jean Cocteau, Simone de Beauvoir, and Lucian Freud—many in the form of pop-ups, scent strips, and other inventive conceits. Although people knew Fleur as a visionary editor, she was also a gifted artist who made incredible paintings and illustrations. She was a real-life **Auntie Mame,** an icon of creativity.

FLAIR

COLLEGE REVIEW ISSUE

August 1950

flair

JANUARY 1951 FIFTY CENTS

NEWS AND IDEAS: The New Year
Guide to London • Fashion Outlook

flair

FLAIR

MAY 1950

THE MONTHLY MAGAZINE
FIFTY CENTS

flair

CHRISTMAS GIVING

DECEMBER 1950 FIFTY CENTS

flair

All Male Issue

July 1950
Fifty cents

FLAIR

Paris Issue
April 1950

The Monthly Magazine
Fifty Cents

Not your grand-mother's vanity: I injected whimsy into a boudoir with a Pedro Friedeberg butterfly chair and a baroque mirror outlined in neon tubing.

OPTICAL ILLUSIONS
Screens and Mirrors

Screens and mirrors are really about smoke and mirrors. Both have the capacity to transform spatial configurations.

mirrors = magic + dazzle

You can never go overboard (or wrong) with reflective surfaces.

Screens often confuse people! But they serve two purposes:

⟜ to break up a space

⟜ to provide a backdrop with visual interest

They are divine for creating spatial separation without making a room seem squashed or overly compartmentalized. They also add a layer of decoration without blocking sight lines. And they are a helluva lot cheaper than a wall!

Embrace the light: Here, I used an eye-catching pair of tri-fold screens to flank a stately sofa, establishing a room within a room and bestowing a strong sense of symmetry and cinematic flair. (See, symmetry is so soothing, no?) Inset mirrored panels bounce sunlight and create the illusion of more windows, which intensifies the brightness.

Back-to-back: Matching Philippe Starck mirrors hung on either side of a vintage screen fashioned from outdoor gates lend just a touch more separation within the open-plan living space of my rad Palm Beach pad.

Give props to screens: It pays to be married to a window dresser: This faux-Warhol screen was a prop from a Barney's display, and now it channels an aura of culteredness in our bedroom. "Real" art can be ridiculously expensive, but there's nothing better than a DIY homage!

A pert pair: Screens cordon off a bookcase-lined hallway between my foyer and living room, carving out an intimate seating area that doubles as a library. The open fretwork pattern cocoons without claustrophobia.

Insta-ARCHITECTURE

Non-built-in features like screens are not just decorative elements; they are what I call "insta-architecture," a means to order a space and lend scale and separation without the need for solid walls. Here are a few ideas for you to steal:

→ Folding screens are versatile pieces: they can be placed against a wall or left freestanding within the middle of a room.

→ Chain-mail curtains similarly create spatial separation *sans* claustrophobia, but with a groovy '70s vibe. • • • • • • • • →

→ Floor mirrors! These are like portals into a magical, faraway land where you are excessively rich and live a luxuriant lifestyle. Use and abuse them.

→ Étagères and double-sided, open-shelved bookcases divide a room in two and offer oodles of extra display space. Lightly accessorize for minimal separation, or load them with books to create a faux wall. They're equally perfect for overly large spaces and studio apartments.

→ Ceiling-mounted drapes. Use these in place of closet doors to provide visual separation between seating vignettes in a large living space or to frame—and close off—an open kitchen.

WORKBOOK
CREATING INSTA-ARCHITECTURE

We all have problematic spaces in our pads that could benefit from a screen or mirror. What elements do you have at your disposal to create a faux wall or inject architectural interest—and where will you use them?

See-through separation: To set off a dining area in the New York townhouse of an art collector, I edged a "floating" marble floor with a curvaceous architectural screen. It strikes just the right balance between separation and enclosure.

A moveable piece: Use a standing mirror to create the illusion of a doorway into another room. A vain faux poodle checking himself out in the mirror is delightfully absurd and fey.

DELUDE YOURSELF: ALWAYS BUY SLIMMING

MIRRORS

125

A double dose: I based this custom vanity on a classical Venetian mirror, adapted into a modern tri-fold style.

Our talented friend: John-Paul Philippe painted the folding screen in our dressing room, where we needed a tall, narrow piece that would fit a sliver of space. The resulting diptych is more art piece than furniture.

Every room needs a dash of **HiPPie** *and a dollop of* **SOCiaLiTe.**

Eclectic is not as easy as you think.
BUT IT'S WORTH IT.

Sequester family photos in large clusters.

There's always room for another lamp. But remember—low wattage for diva lighting.

Let your dogs on the furniture.

Dress up the drywall.
BEFORE PAINTING YOUR WALLS, APPLY GRASSCLOTH WALLPAPER TO ADD TEXTURE.

RESTRaiNT = BOReDOM

STOP, LOOK, *and* REARRANGE.

SCALE!
Mix ginormous with dinky to create dramatic spaces.

Treat your feet to *squishy squishy squishy* **RUGS.**

KiDS' IMaGiNaTiONS THRiVe iN OVeR-DeCORaTeD ROOMS.

FOCAL POINTS

DECORATE WITH KINK.

You may not be an exhibitionist, but your accessories can be.

Wherever your eye wanders it needs an objet d'art.

Think like a

PHOTOGRAPHER.

Look at every vignette in your home like it's being shot for a shelter magazine and style accordingly.

MIRROR EVERYTHING

Mirror adds twinkly glamour, light, and the illusion of space.

PLANTS LIKE TO PARTY.
MAKE DYNAMIC GROUPINGS.

My faves—ficus lyrata, jade plants, and good old orchids.

Minimalism
breeds
Pessimism.

TOO MANY OPINIONS
CAN SPOIL YOUR LOFT.

Trust your gut... and your gay BFF.

LAYER,
LAYER,
LAYER!

IGNORE DISDAINFUL
neighbors...

Pile books everywhere.

LET THE WORLD KNOW YOU'RE SMART.

PHOTO CREDITS

INDEX

131

I believe that your home should make you happy.

I believe that when it comes to decorating, the wife is always right. Unless the husband is gay.

I believe in carbohydrates and to hell with the puffy consequences.

I believe minimalism is a bummer.

I believe handcrafted tchotchkes are life-enhancing.

I believe tassels are the earrings of the home.

I believe in the innate chicness of red with brown.

I believe in being underdressed or overdressed, always.

I believe celebrities should pay full price.

I believe in Palm Beach style: Louis chairs, chinoiserie, Lilly Pulitzer, The Breakers circa '72.

I believe my designs are award-winning even though they've never actually won any.

I believe in Aid to Artisans.

I believe dogs should be allowed in stores and restaurants.

I believe you should throw out your BlackBerry and go pick some actual blackberries.

I believe my lamps will make you look younger and thinner.

I believe in irreverent luxury.